Psalm
Twenty-Three

Illustrated by
Tim Ladwig

EERDMANS BOOKS FOR YOUNG READERS • GRAND RAPIDS / CAMBRIDGE

Dedicated to the children of Newark

–T.L.

Illustrations © 1993 World Impact
Los Angeles, California

First edition © 1993
African American Family Press
An imprint of Multi Media Communicators, Inc.
New York

Scripture taken from the
HOLY BIBLE: NEW INTERNATIONAL VERSION,® NIV.®
Copyright © 1973, 1978, 1984 by the International Bible Society.
Used by permission of Zondervan Bible Publishers and Hodder & Stoughton Limited.

"NIV" is a registered trademark of the International Bible Society.
UK trademark number 1448790

This edition published 1997 by Eerdmans Books for Young Readers
an imprint of Wm. B. Eerdmans Publishing Co.
255 Jefferson Ave. S.E., Grand Rapids, Michigan 49503 /
P.O. Box 163, Cambridge CB3 9PU U.K.

Printed in Hong Kong

02 01 00   7 6 5 4 3

Library of Congress Cataloging-in-Publication Data

Ladwig, Tim.
    Psalm 23 / illustrated by Tim Ladwig.
        p.   cm.
    Originally published: New York: African American Family Press, © 1993.
    Summary: The text of the familiar psalm comparing God to a loving shepherd accompanies illustrations
    which show the world of love and fear faced by an urban African-American family.
    ISBN 0-8028-5160-6 (cloth: alk. paper)
    ISBN 0-8028-5163-0 (pbk: alk. paper)
    1. Bible, O.T. Psalm XXIII—Juvenile literature. [1. Bible. O.T.
    Psalm XXIII. 2. Afro-Americans—Fiction. 3. City and town life—Fiction.] I. Title.
    [BS1450 23rd.L25 1997]
    223'.20520814—dc21   97-14082
                                                CIP
                                                AC
This book was designed by Willem Mineur.
The illustrations were done in watercolor on Fabriano Artistico hot press paper.

ABOUT THE ARTIST

Though he lost an eye as a child, Tim Ladwig gravitated toward the visual arts and learned to draw. His parents encouraged him, supplying him with paper and pencils, and there always seemed to be room on the walls to hang his best work.

In college he studied painting and drawing in Italy and earned a bachelor of arts degree in graphic design from Wichita State University. He learned the mechanics of the graphic arts industry as an illustrator/designer in an advertising agency, where he worked for five years.

For the next fifteen years he labored in the African-American community of Wichita, working as a community minister with World Impact, an inner-city Christian mission. He also worked in Newark and South Central Los Angeles, teaching in teen Bible clubs, working in a reading enrichment program, and assisting in the mission's elementary schools.

While teaching art classes in World Impact's Newark Christian School, Ladwig had a discussion with its principal about the need for culturally accurate children's books for the students. That discussion, followed by conversations with friends about books for urban children, led to the paintings in this book.

Tim Ladwig is married to Leah, his honest critic and chief encourager. They have two daughters, Briana and Makayla, and live in Wichita, Kansas.

PREFACE

City houses jammed together. Streets filled with danger and temptation. Children make their way to school for lessons in the classroom. Children wind their way back home and get lessons in life. And yet, amid such discord stands a safe haven, the small home of an extended family with an abundance of love.

These are just some of the images you see as you leaf through *Psalm Twenty-Three* and view the art work of Tim Ladwig. His is a visual psalm, capturing the ever precarious balance between love and fear that permeates contemporary life in urban America.

The text of the Twenty-Third Psalm was already hundreds of years old when Jesus was born. It contains the prayer of the psalmist, quite possibly King David. When faced with terror, both spiritual and physical, he pictures himself as a sheep and imagines the Lord as the shepherd who will guide him home.

Today the words of the psalmist are thousands of years old, but their message is as moving as ever, and Ladwig's illustrations are fresh and powerful. He depicts a contemporary black family living among urban dangers, a family relying on the Lord as they thread their way through the risk-filled maze of daily life in the city.

In the loving and gifted hands of Ladwig, the book itself becomes an act of devotion, and as you turn its pages and take in the words and the art together, you can hear a prayer for the ages.

This book was previously published in 1993 by African American Family Press. Now it has been completely redesigned, but retains all of Ladwig's original art work.

Psalm
Twenty-Three

The Lord is my shepherd,

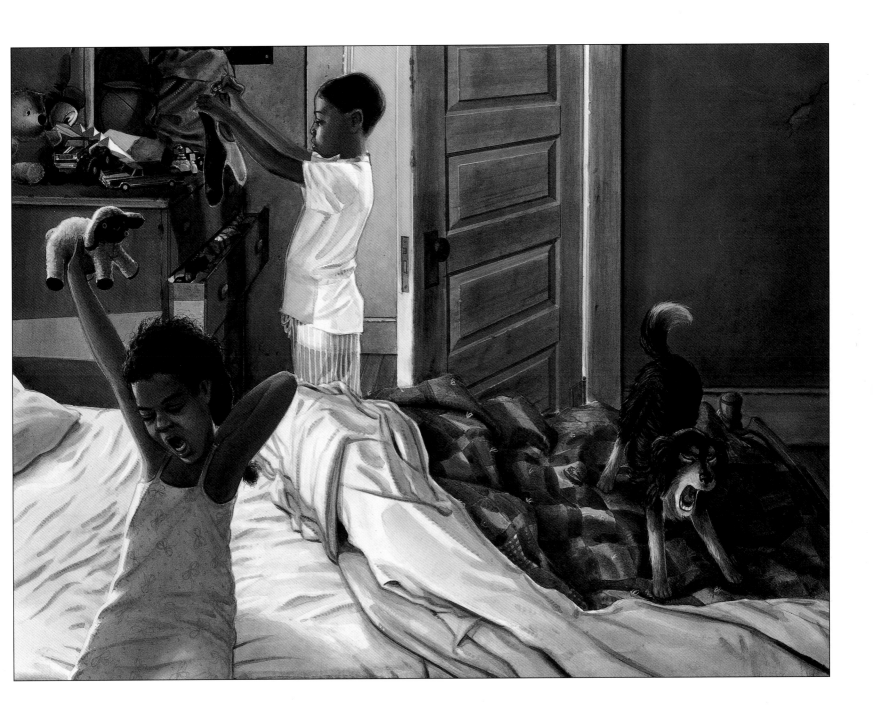

I shall not be in want.

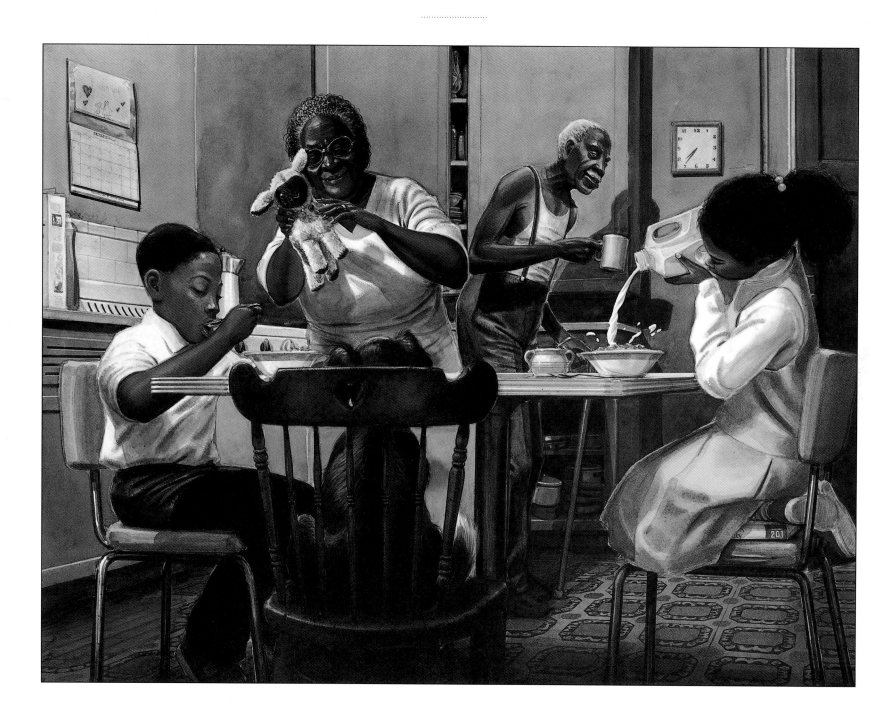

He makes me
lie down in
green pastures,

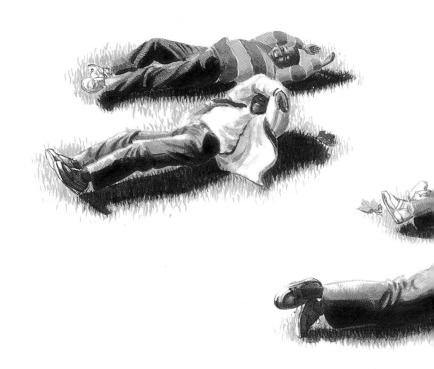

He leads me beside quiet waters,

He restores my soul.

He guides me in paths of righteousness for his name's sake.

Even though I walk through the valley of the shadow of death,

I will fear no evil, for you are with me;

Your rod and your staff, they comfort me.

You prepare a table before me

in the presence of my enemies.

You anoint my head with oil; my cup overflows.

Surely goodness and love will follow me all the days of my life,

And I will dwell
in the house
of the Lord

forever.